Before I Got Here

Before I Got Here

The Wondrous Things We Hear When We Listen to the Souls of Our Children

BLAIR UNDERWOOD

photographs by Donyell Kennedy-McCullough

ATRIA BOOKS
1230 Avenue of the Americas
New York, NY 10020

ISBN-13: 978-0-7432-7149-3
ISBN-10:   0-7432-7149-1

First Atria Books hardcover edition October 2005

Designed by Joel Avirom, Jason Snyder, and Meghan Day Healey

10 9 8 7 6 5 4

ATRIA BOOKS is a trademark of Simon & Schuster, Inc.

Manufactured in the United States of America

For information regarding special discounts for bulk purchases, please contact Simon & Schuster Special Sales at 1-800-456-6798 or business@simonandschuster.com

Blair Underwood:

For my bride, Desiree,
and our three miracles, Paris, Brielle, and Blake.

Thank you for sharing this brief,
shining lifetime with me.

Donyell Kennedy-McCullough:

For my parents, Bill and Therese White,
my husband Suli,
and the two amazing spirits that fuel me
Kennedy-Rue and Nahzi!!

And lastly, for my MeMe . . . my guardian angel.

about the photographs

by Donyell Kennedy-McCullough

We'd like to thank the children—our friends and our own—who allowed us to photograph them for this book. While their images don't correspond to the words quoted and stories told in these pages, they do complement the amazing things our children say and in another way reveal how deep are the souls of our children.

acknowledgments

First, I'd like to express my deepest gratitude to the village that helped bring this project to fruition. Being fortunate enough to have a book published is, as my mother always says, "more than a notion."

My family sustains and astonishes me each and every day. Profound thanks are due my wife, Desiree, for always believing in me, supporting me, and tolerating the spirit of stubbornness that on occasion abducts her unsuspecting husband.

To my son, Paris, whose innocence and wide-eyed perspective of our universe served as the inspiration for this book, thank you.

Thank you to my daughter, Brielle, and my son, Blake, for constantly providing a glimpse inside the purity of their souls.

Thanks so much to my cousin Lynne (Tita) Andrews for being such a nurturing and positive influence in the lives of our children. You've been there since day one with each child and you are a tremendous blessing in our home. Desi and I thank God for you, every day.

To Diane DaCosta, your persistence and determination to

achieve inspires me to be better. . . at everything. Thank you for showing me that having a book published is not only a possibility and/or probability, but indeed a reality.

Also, heartfelt thanks to Donyell Kennedy-McCullough, who after sharing personal accounts of her amazing child encouraged me to compile similar anecdotes and create *Before I Got Here*. Thank you, Donyell, for the extra push.

A special thanks to my agent, Manie Barron, who tirelessly trudged through the rain-soaked city of New York to eventually find the perfect publishing company for us.

It is absolutely more than a notion, to find a publishing house that not only sees your vision but embraces it. For that, I will forever be indebted to my editor, Malaika Adero, my publisher, Judith Curr, and the entire staff at Atria Books. Thank you for your patience and enthusiasm during this creative phase. God bless you.

Tananarive Due and Steven Barnes, I am honored to call you

friends. Thank you for your insight and wealth of knowledge as I embark upon this foray into the literary world.

Thank you to the Owens family for your example of faith and family.

Thanks to Danita Patterson for your spiritual guidance and perpetual "golden moments."

Thanks to my grand godchildren Blair Brittney, Alexia Grace, and Kenny Fields, Jr. Though I don't see you as often as I would like, I am forever grateful for the light that shines within you.

Chinue Wells, thank you for your joyful spirit and hard work in attempting to wrangle me for a photo shoot.

Thank you to my manager, Ron West, for everything, but specifically for the idea to create a website. Without an outreach vehicle such as our website, it would have been much more difficult to amass our many stories.

Thanks to Damien Smith for constructing the website and providing our cyberspace link to the world.

Thank you to Denise Ruiz for helping out on our photo shoot. You are a calming spirit and a blessing to all you encounter.

Thank you to Elisa Rudder for being my guardian angel.

Finally, as always, I give thanks to my extraordinary family who have supported me throughout my life: my father, Col. Frank Underwood, Sr.; my mother, Marilyn Ann Underwood; my brother, Frank Underwood, Jr.; my sisters, Marlo Collins and Mellisa Anne Underwood. I thank you all for your undying love, honesty, candidness and for always believing I can, even when I may think I cannot.

The many contributors and friends of this project, too numerous to name, have encouraged and inspired me by embracing the belief that these "vibrations of light" we call children are indeed worthy of our utmost.

Ultimately, as Kahlil Gibran reminds us, their souls dwell in the house of tomorrow.

—*Blair Underwood*

First and foremost, I would like to give special thanks to those who birthed my creativity, my parents Bill and Therese White and Arthur Washington.

I would also like to thank those who continue to inspire me: my husband Suli, whom I can't thank enough for being so loving and supportive of the craziness I have labeled creativity.

Thank you to one of the most phenomenal spirits to grace my life: my daughter Kennedy-Rue. You make me believe that the world is so much bigger than here and now. Thank you for choosing me.

And my son, Nahzi: thank you for challenging my fears.

Thank you, Blair, for being such an amazing spirit and being! You are truly a light and those of us who are fortunate to know you are forever blessed. Thank you for your friendship! Desiree Underwood, beauty begets beauty. Thank you for sharing your gifts.

To my special angel Jada Pinkett Smith, thank you for believing in me and pushing me ever so gently to recognize my calling and embrace my highest self. I will be eternally grateful to you for not giving me an out!

Will, thanks for setting the example for your friends and encouraging us all to do things that ensure that the world is a better place because we were here! I HEARD YOU! THANK YOU!!!

Thank you to my oldest and dearest friends Leslie Perry and Stephen Perry. My goddaughters Morgan, Lauren, and Cameron Perry; Jaime King for always being so forthright and my reality check; Michelle Listenbee-Brown for the years of friendship and the gift of my godson Noah. Daphne Wayans, how can I thank you enough for teaching me the true spirit of motherhood?! Thank you, thank you, thank you! Tisha Campbell-Martin, you continue to inspire me with your words and your deeds. Kebe Dunn, you keep me in touch with the universe's energy; Annabeth White, thank you for the lesson of truth. Tammy Garnes, thank you for all of your love and support; Kimberly Frelow (we go so far back

it's scary), thank you for believing in me no matter how far-fetched the idea! Olivia Riley-Williams, "The Baby" grew up!
Thank you for always supporting my crazy ventures. Lisa Bonner, thank you for all of your hard work in making sure that this project came to fruition.

Thank you to all of my friends: Lorna the Entertainer, Holly Peete, Nicole Murphy, Regina King, Duane Martin, Tichina Arnold, Lauris Freeman, Julissa Marquez, Alex Thomas, Stacey Mathew, Christopher Spencer, Darrel Heath, Brooklyn McLinn, Eriq LaSalle, Dominique and Prophet Jennings, Terry Christanio, Shelli Alexander, Wendi Mathew, Jamie Carmody, Jana Babatunde-Bey, Elizabeth Woods, Gina Harris—you all keep me going!

To my sisters—Tonya Nickerson, Meisha Washington, Shelia Washington, and Andrea Avery—thanks for the laughs.

My sisters- and brothers-in-law—Sayeeda Asha-Camp, Davia Moore, Shahid Brown, and Hassan McCullough—I love you!

I would like to add a special thanks to my agent John Silbersack for tireless dedication to making this project possible!

My mother-in-law, Betty Moore, thank you for your love and support.

My aunts Ann Kennedy, Marilyn Moten, Debra English, Aunt Shelia, Aunt Sadiqa and Auntie Gaye.

To my grandfather Merlin R. Kennedy: Thank you providing the foundation.

Lastly, thank you to all of the children who have allowed me to photograph them!!! You are truly my inspiration.

—*Donyell Kennedy-McCullough*

Before I Got Here

It has been said that **we are not human beings having a spiritual experience, but rather, we are SPIRITUAL beings having a human experience.**

As our three children, ages eight, six, and three, practically ransacked my parents' home during a recent visit, I would often glance

Introduction Blair by Underwood

over and steal a glimpse of either my mother or father in virtual bliss as they witnessed the near demolition of their living quarters. The same acts that would have landed me in "Punishment Purgatory" bring sheer delight to grandparents and, at rare times, to parents. When I asked

my father why he was so joyful in the presence of his grandchildren, he began to wax philosophical on the inexplicable emotions one feels when face-to-face with their legacy. He then commented on how happy our children seemed. He said, "That means you guys are doing your jobs right as parents."

I consider this to be the ultimate compliment. Though my profession is that of an actor, the monikers I cherish most are Husband *and* Father.

I feel that, as parents, we are blessed to be entrusted with the lives of our children, these tiny angels from above. We are the guardians, for too brief a time, of these souls that are very much alive and well-defined when they relocate among us.

When each of our children was born, I witnessed my wife

bring forth new life. The first birth was by cesarean. With the subsequent births I watched as she reached down, placed her hands under the armpits of our babies, and literally pulled them into the world, without the use of any drugs.

From the instant a newborn takes its initial breath, it is evident that the basic foundation and/or blueprint of that baby's personality is already in place.

Though operating on instinct when babies find their way to their mother's nipple to suckle for the first time, there are already subtle clues about the persons they will become. **Even in their earliest weeks here, there are signs of the persona yet to emerge . . . if we only pay attention.** Consequently I feel that parents have very little control of what type of child (physically, mentally, etc.) will be divinely assigned to us.

On the other hand, far too many influences lay in wait with the sole intent to corrupt the purity of children's souls. In our own attempts to be worthy of the title "parent," we endeavor, at times, to control, protect, guide, expose, teach, and "let go." "Let go," to allow our children to evolve, mature, and eventually replenish the earth with their own seeds. Ah, yes, the proverbial "Circle of Life."

But, at what point does the circle begin, and where, if ever, if ever does it end?

Where do our souls begin and where do they end?

I believe in the "eternal perspective" of life. In other words, life does not begin and end on our planet Earth. There is a continuum of our life force that inherently remembers thoughts, sights, and sounds of a previous existence . . . *"before we got here."*

Where, when, and how we existed prior to now is both impossible to know and irrelevant. What is enormously relevant is the fact that *we are given brief glimpses into this other world by the purest of beings, our children. They visit and share our space for just a finite period.* They walk among us so innocent and naive, yet profoundly wise and insightful. Somehow they are still connected to that "other place" that is, by definition, the manifestation of love eternal.

As a father of three young children, I have experienced firsthand the silliness, the elation, the bickering, and the exploration of new worlds through infant eyes. **The occasional nonchalant "utterings" of those youngsters can now and then leave a parent speechless . . . if we truly listen to what our children are telling us.**

8   Blair **Underwood**

A few years ago, when my eldest son was four years old, he discovered the concept of "jokes." He was absolutely fascinated by the mechanics of a joke. What made it funny, why do people laugh, how does one "deliver" a joke?

I explained to him that, oftentimes, a joke is funny because of its punch line or "button." Usually the button has a double meaning or double entendre. **So, after I'd discussed this with him, as you can well imagine, *double entendre* became the phrase of the day.**

Later that evening, while driving to the airport, I noticed that my son was very introspective while staring out of the window. I asked him what he was thinking about and he proceeded to tell me about a dream that he'd had, "last night."

"Oh, hey, Daddy, 'last night' means the last night a few nights ago and it means the *last* night when there are no more mornings and no more nights."

Only half listening, preoccupied with so many other daily demands, I offered an obligatory grunt of affirmation, to assure him that Daddy was indeed listening. I continued to drive and after a while, I replayed, in my head, what my son had said. I asked him to repeat it, and this time he elaborated: "... the *last* night when there are no more mornings and no more nights, and that is when all of the people go up to Heaven. 'Last night' has two meanings, Daddy, it's a 'double entendre.' Isn't that cool?"

By now, I had almost collided with the car in front of me, so I pulled over when I realized that he was referring to "The Last Days" and to what is referred to by biblical scholars as "The Rapture." This is considered to be when all "believers" will ascend to Heaven. Since he was only four, I can't imagine I would have shared this concept with my son yet, because

Blair Underwood

conversations about death or leaving the comfort of home and family can be disconcerting to a young child.

Because I was raised by parents who encouraged artistic, personal, and spiritual expression, I feel it is essential that I, even as a relatively new parent, afford my children the same freedom. So I asked him who had told him such things.

"God told me, when he made me, but I only had one ear at the time, so I could only hear a little."

Was this an "utterance" from a child's vivid imagination, the result of incessant, religious brainwashing (as one obviously bitter and angry gentleman recently wrote to me), or was it an actual eyewitness account of a soul's emergence into "being"... the recollections of its own creation?

When I shared this story with friends and family, I soon found that other parents or caregivers had similar stories. One

friend, in particular, Donyell Kennedy-McCullough, urged me to compile the stories and put them into a book. Not only does Donyell have brilliant ideas, she is also a gifted photographer. The artistic images of children that you will see in the following pages were all captured by the lens of Donyell's camera.

We in Western civilization live in a time when there is a reawakening and thirst for an understanding of spiritual connectedness. Simultaneously **parents are constantly seeking avenues to familial connectedness, and more specifically, a means to understanding their own children.** There is much conversation about Metagifted Education, i.e., the Children of the New Earth, the New Children, the Indigo Children etc.

I've never professed to be an expert in child psychology and I do not represent myself here as such. **What I am is a perpetual student of life, as it unfolds before me in the form of my bride Desiree and the three miracles to whom she has given birth.** As an observer, I've already found that, as these children grow older, either their ability to remember diminishes or their reluctance to expound increases. What a magnificent gift our world has been given through the children. If not encouraged and nurtured, we will eventually squander these golden opportunities to glimpse another existence and possibly our future.

This book is about encouraging all of us, not only parents, to listen to the "little people" around us. It is not about any particular religion or dogma. It is about opening our eyes to see and our ears to hear the tiny miracles among us, called children. As we live our lives, struggling to survive, trying to make sense of the chaos of the day, it will be infinitely rewarding to take time once in a while and listen to a child's soul.

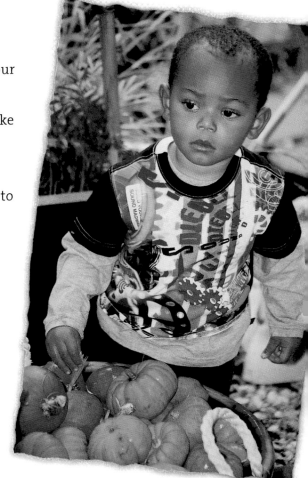

My mother died when my son Brandon was just five years old. We were very close to her, and hers was a sudden death. I really struggled with how I was going to tell Brandon that Nana had gone to Heaven. When I picked him up from day care after her death, I just sat him down on my lap and told him what had happened. My beautiful son leaned back and looked up into my eyes with a look that conveyed *What's the big deal?* He said **"Mommy, Nana isn't gone!! All you have to do is rub your heart, and there she is!!"** And he demonstrated by rubbing his heart and giving me the most beautiful smile ever. He was, and continues to be, the most precious and amazing person in my life.

—JoAnne Villa

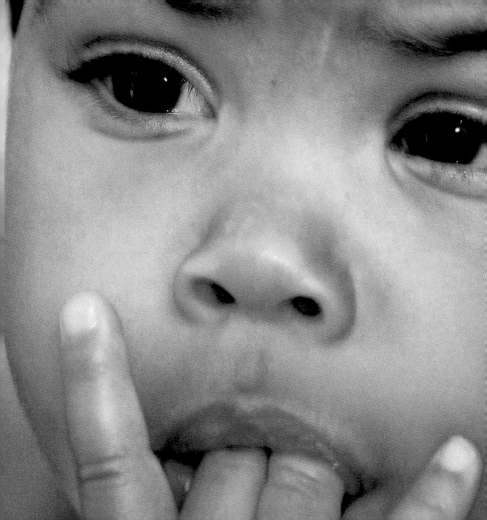

My youngest daughter, Kacie, and I were walking outside the apartment one day, when we discovered a large group of caterpillars in the middle of the street. While many others were crawling around in the safe confines of the surrounding landscape, these caterpillars in the street ran the risk of an untimely demise. *Kacie looked at me as an occasional vehicle would go by, turning her head away so she wouldn't see one of those fuzzy little crawlers meeting its end.* As soon as the road was clear we picked up and relocated as many of them as we could to a safer haven.

Then we came across another amazing sight. Several of these caterpillars had started their remarkable transformation of becoming something even more beautiful. Many cocoons were hanging from the eaves of the building on their way to becoming butterflies. To make a long story short, it was that look from my daughter's big, beautiful brown eyes that reminds me just how precious life is. Even with all the hustle and bustle of our busy adult lives, we all need to stop, look, and listen to what our children's souls are telling us.

—Terence McNulty

While getting ready for church one day, I was strapping on a new pair of platform sandals (very vogue at the time). My little three-year-old daughter, Truly, looked at me, and we had the following conversation:

TRULY: Mommy, I like your shoes.

ME: Well, thank you, Truly.

TRULY: I used to have shoes like that.

ME: You did? When?

TRULY: **Before I came to you.**

Blair Underwood

ME: What do you mean, before you came to me?

TRULY: I was a mommy, too, before I came to you.

With that, she went scampering out of the room in search of more things to explore. Needless to say, the hair on my arms, legs, and back of my neck were standing straight up, and they still do when I tell this story. She was always the perfect little girl and still is the perfect daughter. A mommy couldn't wish for more, and **she obviously learned well in her other life as a mommy.**

—Jolyne Roberts

have always been extremely close to my grandson, Wes. Even at the hospital on the day he was born, we gazed deeply into each other's eyes; this connection was instant and continues to this day. When he was about two years old and just learning to put sentences together, we had a conversation about my father, his great-grandfather (who he refers to as Grampa). **My father died eleven years prior to Wes coming to us, so Wes had never had a chance to meet him. Of course, I thought they'd never meet.**

Little did I know that Wes already knew his great-grandfather. This is how he told me: One day as we were on our way out the door, we passed a picture collage in the hallway. Wes made me stop and pointed to a picture of his

great-grandfather. I had never pointed him out to him simply because I thought Wes was too young to understand who he was. Wes looked at that picture, and we had the following conversation:

WES: Look, Gramma, there's Grampa!

ME: That's right, Wes, but how did you know it was Grampa?

WES: Because he comes and sits on my bed every night.

ME: He does? Why does he sit on your bed?

WES: He tells me stories at night, and he stays with me until I fall asleep.

Wes is now six and still tells us about his grandpa and how he visits him. **He says Grampa doesn't visit him every night like he used to because he's very busy where he is.** We keep Grampa alive in Wes by talking about him often, and Wes will always tell us when he visited him last. He's not frightened by him; he knows he's very loved by a great-grandfather who will always be with him.

—Jolyne Roberts

One night while my wife and I were fixing dinner, our three-year-old daughter, Izabella, stood on a chair watching us. My wife hugged me and started to kiss me. I pulled away from her jokingly, saying, "I shouldn't be kissing you because I'm a virgin."

Izabella looked at me with a serious face and said, **"Poppa, you're not a virgin, Mommy has my little brother in her stomach."** We stood there in shock. We bought a pregnancy test and found out that my wife was pregnant. The doctor confirmed that she was due in late March of 2004.

—**Julian Torrez**

It goes without saying that when my son is hurt or crying, I rush to pick him up and console him. **In the two short years of his life I've had to do a lot of consoling, as most moms do.** But one day the tables were turned, and I was blessed with a glimpse into my child's soul. This was during a very bad time in my life when I was struggling with the onset of single-motherhood and trying to do the best I could to provide for my son.

One especially difficult evening, as I lay in bed rocking my son to sleep, I began to weep. It was such a deep and heartfelt cry that I could hardly catch my breath. As I cried, *I silently prayed to God to help me with my struggles and to bless my son with health and happiness,* and I asked that He help me be a better mom. As I finished my prayer, my two-year-old son, who could not yet speak any words, arose from my lap and cupped my face with both hands. He raised my face so that I could see him looking directly into my eyes. **At that moment my son had the most angelic smile on his face and he looked at me, not like a child normally looks at you, but as if he were reading my thoughts.** He lifted my chin and kissed me very gently and then again, smiled. I was overcome with peace in an instant. Suddenly I knew that everything was okay and that my prayers had been answered. My son then lay back down and went to sleep, as if he had never been awake.

I first wondered where my son could have learned to console and bring peace to me. But the more I have thought about that night, and that moment, I have come to believe that it was a "soulful" moment, something you can't truly understand until you have experienced it firsthand. When you do, you'll know.

—**Chimene Gould**

When my son Aaron was four and a half years old he was playing a computer game when, out of the blue, he stopped and said, "Mom, I have a brother who already died and is in Heaven."

"How do you know that, Aaron?" I asked.

"I just do," he said.

I then told Aaron about a miscarriage I had in the past and that we didn't know if the baby was a boy or girl (we had never told him about it before). He replied "Yeah, that was my brother . . . he's in Heaven now." He then went back to playing his computer game.

—Jennie Petrovich

One day, years ago, my two-year-old was working hard driving his tricycle around my yardwork tools on our large cement driveway, entirely engaged in the task at hand. When he stopped, I heard silence and glanced his way. *He looked at me with his "old soul" look and a twinge of anxiety.* Standing over his trike and pointing at the sliver of moon shining in the late Georgia afternoon sky, he exclaimed, "Look, Daddy, a broken moon!" I smiled to myself at his concern and this new perspective I had never before heard.

I soothingly asked him, "Ty, you've seen the moon before, haven't you?"

He looked at me expectantly with those big blue eyes and said, **"Yes, Daddy, but how did it get broke? Is this bad?"** There it was, one of those moments of truth for a parent; my young son had never seen anything but the full moon and now he felt threatened by a universe gone awry. I wondered if *broken* to him meant that light was failing. ***Or had the moon been broken into slivers and bits by a giant sledgehammer in the sky,*** which would soon be a threat to us. As I squatted beside him to reassure him, I contemplated the limits of my version of two-year-old vocabulary in explaining the universe to a soul wary enough to sense these dangers. Or could the universe be explained to an old soul with a hug?

—John Ennis

My youngest son, Cameron, once asked me why grown-ups don't just stop working so hard all the time and play a little bit every day, since adults worry so much about grown-up stuff. His exact four-year-old quote was, " . . . 'Cause when you play you don't have to think very hard or worry . . . you have fun."

—Nicole Hoppman

Blair **Underwood**

As a young child, I was never told that I was white. I was in a state of ignorance about color, for which I thank my mother to this day. As a consequence, the notion of telling my children that they are white (and therefore that other people in the world are different) had never occurred to me. So when my four-year-old son Steven asked me what color he was, I was almost lost as to what to say. *Should I give him the P.C. term* Caucasian, *something sure to* *confuse him? Or should I give him the easier word, white?* He would surely understand that word, but we had been through not mixing the different paint colors, and if I told him that he was like one of his paints would I not be telling him subtly that he was not to "mix" with any other colors? It turns out that I was completely overreacting. For as soon as the response "What color do you think you are?" came out of my mouth he turned up to me and said, **"Can't you see? I'm Steven-colored!"**

—LeAnn Wood

More than twenty years ago there was a memorable television commercial for peanut butter. There was a jingle that went, "If you believe in peanut butter, clap your hands," and then there were three claps. At church one Sunday, the congregation was talking about television and how it influences our lives and what we believe and don't believe.

One little girl raised her hand and said **"On TV there's a commercial that asks you to clap your hands if you believe in peanut butter.** That's the difference between God and peanut butter. **To believe in God you don't have to clap your hands."** This was from a five-year-old. There wasn't a dry adult eye in the room.

—David Pierce

Rachel was two years old when I was her nanny. My grandmother had died over the past weekend. I had been very close to her and was very sad. **I did not talk about my *vovoa* (Portuguese for "grandmother") with Rachel, nor did I mention my sadness, but she must have been able to sense it.** That morning as I was dressing her, she asked, "Do you have a grandma?"

"No, honey, all my grandparents are dead, I don't have any at all," I replied.

Without missing a beat she said, *"Oh, but they're not gone, they're still living."*

"What do you mean?"

"They live in your memory, so you can always go and see them."

I thought at that moment my *vovoa* was smiling down on me, and I haven't been lonely for her ever since.

—Sarah Mello

At the age of two, our daughter, Katelyn, was very talkative; her thoughts and vocabulary were already well developed. We talked with her, but mostly we listened. One evening when she was playing "alone" in her bedroom, I went into her room to see what she was doing. When I asked her what she was up to she responded, **"I'm listening to Papaw. He's in my rocker."** Papaw is our name for her great-grandfather, who had died when she was only three months old. He was a remarkable man who had spent time with Katelyn in her first few

Blair **Underwood**

months of life. She was the only one of his children, grandchildren, or great-grandchildren he had ever held at such a young age. **He had never held any of his five daughters at a young age as he felt they were too fragile.** But he had held Katelyn. He had smiled. She is still comforted in the fact that he has a special place in her heart and she had often said that he was here again to visit her. *At the age of eight, she still remembers.* When questioned, she says he doesn't visit much anymore, but she still feels he is "with her."

—**Kathy Clark**

I am a single mother of two boys who are three years apart. When my mother, who was my best friend, passed in 1993, my boys were three and six years old. They asked a lot of questions about her dying. Mikie, who is the older child, asked while looking at her in the casket, "Mom, is Grandma asleep? We should wake her!" **It was hard for me to explain to a six-year-old, but I told him she was like Sleeping Beauty and had to go to another place.** I didn't let them see her being put into the ground, because I know there would have been more questions. Several months later, while immersed in a moment remembering my mother, I started to cry.

My younger son, Brandon, who was three years old, was nearby and started to pat me on the back. He asked in an adult tone of voice, "Why is you crying, Mom? What's wrong?"

I told him that I really missed my mom and her smile.

He answered back to me, in a way I would never forget, **"Don't cry, Mom. I'll be your mother!"** and he smiled exactly the way she used to smile at me. A feeling came over me, and I hugged him tighter than ever, and my tears went away. Until this day, I still feel a soul and spiritual connection with my mother through my children.

—Brenda Ward

My son just turned four years old this past June, and has been attending King Baptist Preschool for over a year now. **His father and I have been divorced for two years, and he spends some weekends with his father. When he came home from one of those weekend trips he carefully looked around the house.** Not finding what he was searching so hard for, he finally asked me, "Mom, did you get something for me?"

I was a little surprised and asked him what he expected me to get him.

He said, **"Well, Dad always buys me something."** I told him that I bought him things also. It may not be a toy or clothes all of the time, but food and shelter were important, too.

My four-year-old son didn't miss a beat and very seriously informed me, "Well, Mom, God said that if you give to me, you will receive blessings. *I guess you just don't want your blessings, huh, Mom?"*

—Latonia Smith

My four-year-old daughter looks up at my husband and myself with her big blue eyes and says that she remembers when we were little kids. We tell her that she was still in the sky with God when we were little. *She tells us that she remembers us playing with our mommies and daddies and she remembers how happy we were when we were little* like she is now. It makes us both think about how big her blue eyes and heart really are. Little kids can remember things that we cannot. They are not tainted by the world's stress. They see only what their big eyes and heart let them see— not what we tell them to see.

—Veronica Kampelman

My seven-year-old daughter Savannah, my four-year-old daughter Annaliese, and I were driving on the way to Gramma's house. We were discussing their father Van and me as teenagers. As the conversation progressed, **confusion set upon Annaliese as to whether or not she had been born at the time Van and I first started dating**. After trying to explain to her that some of our dating happened before she was born, my adult explanation only confused her more. Savannah, who had been quietly listening, said, "You know, Annaliese, back when we were just thoughts in God's heart."

And to that, Annaliese replied with full understanding of "that" time and said . . . *"Oh yeah, I remember."* One must stop to think of what it is that children know that we as adults only wish we could fathom. **—Mellissa King**

While conversing with my eldest son Garyson, a three-year-old at the time, I listened to him tell me about the puppies his grandmother's dog had recently given birth to. We told him that he could go pick out a puppy, which he gladly did. Running back into the house, he looked up to me and said, "Dad, I picked out my favorite one."

Seeing the excitement and joy in his face, and not knowing at the time if the puppy was male or female, I asked, "Garyson, what are you going to name it?" He looked at me with a very serious look, and, as if I was supposed to know, he said "Favorite!" Now, how's that for hearing, and at the same time not listening, to a child?

—**Gary Walker**

My six-year-old "remembers" a lot from the time before she was born. She told me about how she chose my husband and me.

I asked her why, out of all the mommies and daddies, she chose to be our child, and she said, **"Because I knew that we needed to be together."** So I asked her if she had her choice of any parents she wanted, and she said, "Yes, we all do."

■

My dad died nearly eleven years ago, and of course our girls never had the opportunity to meet him, but Sarah knows him. I asked her how it is that she misses him when she never met him.

She said, "Oh, I did meet him, Mommy."

"When did you meet him?" I asked

"When I was up in Heaven. He used to play with me, and I would sit on his lap and he would tell me things about when you were a little girl."

I asked her what he looked like, and she said, **"He looks like you."**

■

Sarah tells me about when she was in my tummy. She says that she remembers being warm and cozy, and that she was very happy in there. This past May, she said to me "Mom, Luis's dad is a doctor, I think you should speak to him." (Luis is a little school friend of hers.)

"Why? Do you think I'm sick?" I asked.

"No, Mommy, of course you're not sick. *You have a baby in your tummy*." She giggled.

"No, sweetie, there is not a baby in Mommy's tummy. Why do you say that? Do you think my tummy looks big?" I smiled.

"No, but I do know there is a baby in there, and you should see the doctor." Well, lo and behold I was late and when I performed a home pregnancy test the results came positive! I was stunned!

Later, when we spoke to the girls about it, Sarah said, **"See, I was right. I knew our baby was here."**

Unfortunately, I lost the baby when I was three months pregnant.

Sarah and Lucinda, my four-year-old, tried to comfort me. Lucinda said, "I am sad about our baby going back to Heaven. I was going to be a big sister. I had a lot of things to teach our baby."

Sarah said, "I'm very sad that our baby wasn't strong enough to stay, but at least now we will have our very own angel up in Heaven, and Grandaddy will be happy to have one of his grandkids with him to keep him company. He will really like that."

I had tears running down my cheeks and when the girls noticed I was crying they said, "Are you sad about the baby?"

"Yes, but also sad because I know that this is painful for you both and that makes me sad for you," I said.

"It's okay, Mommy, don't be sad," Sarah said. "The baby will come back when it's ready. It wasn't time right now. I am sad, but it's not like it's the end of the world or anything."

—Jackie Diamond

Shortly after my father died, Lazaro, my grandson (we call him Laz), would go up to the front picture window and **put his little arms up in the air to be picked up by someone who wasn't there.** Laz was only sixteen months old and would just stand there with his arms reaching up to the top of the curtains, looking up into something, and then he'd put his hands down and go about his business. **This would go on continually.**

Today, Laz is four and he's constantly telling me about my father. He can tell me so many details about my father, it is as if my dad's spirit is in him. It just touches my heart, blows me away, and always leaves me smiling.

—Lazaro

Around five years ago our family went through a particularly difficult time. **My husband and I were newly separated, and all of the chaos surrounding our decision to separate had taken permanent residence in each of our lives:** my husband's, our two sons', and mine. During one of the lowest points of that period, my then eight-year-old son Cole and I took our dog Jack for a walk on a silent but brilliantly starry night. Looking for some sign of hope or encouragement, I looked up at the stars and was reminded of my Creator, sighed, and said aloud, "Well, Cole, one thing that we do know is that if God can hold the stars, He can most certainly hold our lives . . ."

With only a few seconds' hesitation, Cole grabbed my hand and joined me in my Heavenward gaze and then said, "Actually, Mom, if God can hold our lives, He can easily hold the stars." Since that starry night and that season of desolation in our family, **my marriage has been restored and my family joyfully reunited**. And in those moments when I think upon yesterday's famine and today's plenty, I am reminded of the honest words that once flowed from an eight-year-old sage—words that compelled me to go on believing, hoping, trusting, rejoicing, and knowing.

—**Nicole Walters**

My children's father and I had just separated, which caused chaos in our home for a while. One morning, as my oldest daughter, Ceira, then five years old, was tying her shoes before school and I was getting ready for work, she said, **"You know God loves us, right?"**

I said, "Sure He does, honey. Why do you say that?"

She replied, "Because He tells me all the time." As she stood up looking at me nonchalantly, she said, "He's holding my hand right now."

I was just flooded with warmth, and knew that God, our comforter, was with us.

—Lorissa Owens

At about two and a half years old, my son, AJ, kept saying things that made me pause and wonder. One such thing was "When I was a little girl . . ." I finally decided, when he was about three, that I would ask him what he meant, but I didn't know how to approach it. I finally decided that a direct question was the best way to handle it, so I asked him, "Who were you before you were you?" He responded, "I was a little girl, Mommy." **—Alexandria Piland**

I was reading a book about angels, and there was a picture of an angel on the front cover. My son came into the room, and seeing the picture, he said, "That is the thing outside my window at night protecting me."

—Itai Mcintyre

My son's name, Akil, means intelligent. I must admit that as a single mom I am not always listening to him and not always attuned to what he feels. I remember one occasion when there was something he wanted—I don't remember what in particular—and I said no, but then I said maybe. He said "*Maybe* is just a baby that needs *love* until it says *yes*."

"What does that mean?" I asked him. He explained that **I just needed some time and love from him to make me say yes.** I am still amazed about how right he was. Like babies, we need love, and in time that love turns us from maybe to yes. I have decided that when I die that is what will go on my headstone.

—Ingrid Dudley

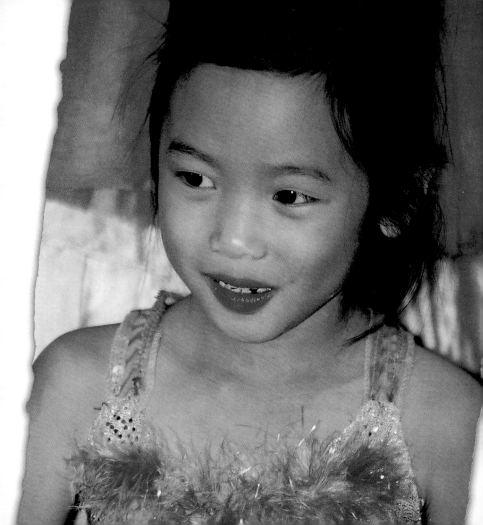

My name is Dinneen, and I am in my early thirties. When I was about three or four I stunned my father one evening at a Japanese restaurant, Hydee-O. I always enjoyed eating at that restaurant, and when we did eat there, **my father was amazed that such a young child could have such agility with chopsticks and a love for sushi.** One evening, at Hydee-O, my father said to me, "In a past life you must have been a Japanese princess."

I said bluntly and with confidence and conviction, "No, Dad, a Japanese cat."

—Dinneen Coster

During a recent and very trying time, I was sitting in my angel room crying. My three-year-old grandson came in and said to me, **"Trust and believe in the Lord your God and He shall comfort you."**

I looked at him, startled, and said, "What did you say, Sebastian?" He repeated it verbatim. My baby has never stepped one foot inside a church. His mother, my daughter, is not religious, nor does she speak of God. And yet there are divinely connected children, possessing Godly wisdom beyond their years.

It is imperative that we nurture their souls, encourage their paths and bring them together with those of like minds. They must be protected. "We never forget or lose the 'blueprint' of our souls," as the angel children remind us. We become cluttered and obstructed by illusions, fears, and false belief systems imposed upon us. Eventually, when we discover that illusion no longer satisfies the souls' truths, we return to our search. *We seek the Spirit of Truth—the Holy Spirit—that lives within each and every soul alive.* This Spirit allows our voices to be heard and encourages us to speak, not from fear, but from our souls' truths.

—April Colon

My niece, Riley, is three years old. As she awoke one morning, she turned to me, sat up, and said, **"I have to tell you four important things: I have a dog named Kelly, a cat named Elizabeth, and a horse named Sam. They live in my big blue house."** She proceeded to describe what they looked like. She doesn't have a dog or a horse, but my cat is named Elizabeth.

Soon after, my cat, who was twenty years old, had to be put to sleep. Riley had seen her a couple of times, but seemed to know that she would soon be going back to the "big blue house" (Heaven). **It was the combination of her sitting up so abruptly after having been so sound asleep, and her wide-eyed expression** as she said she had "four very important things" to tell me that make me think she was recollecting something from an earlier but real time.

—Cynthia Shea

74   Blair Underwood

One day, as I was repairing the plumbing at the home of some clients, their four-year-old son came into the bathroom to watch me work. I was under the sink, lying awkwardly, with my head in the cabinet and one arm holding a wrench on a pipe as I groped outside of the cabinet for a tool. **Suddenly the four-year-old boy handed me a tool. I then reached out and before I could decide what I needed next, a tool was again handed to me.** I then realized, *a four-year-old just anticipated and handed me tools*. I came out from under the sink and looked at the smiling little chocolate face, and I said, "Jamall, thank you for helping me, but how did you know what tool to hand me?"

"I used to do this kind of work when I was a man."

"When was that, Jamall?" I asked.

"When I was here before."

I was so surprised that I could not keep a straight face. I tried to think of what else to ask. Could this child really have been alive here on earth before, and remember it? As I searched for another question, **the little boy looked at me as if he had said something wrong and he then got up and ran away.** That began my asking clients to tell me if their three- or four-year-olds say things that are surprising. I hear quite a lot of stories.

—Leon Watts III

As we celebrated my coworker's birthday, my colleagues and I sat around and shared stories. The conversation led to profound words spoken by one of my coworker's sons. When he was two years old, he said to her, "I got to pick you for my mommy, out of all the mommies."

—Tammie

Each child is unique, and God uses each in more ways than one. I can only cry at times or just shake my head in amazement at how He works and how He gets messages and reminders of hope to me through children—**especially my six-year-old granddaughter, Tamia. That child is something else.** I sing in a gospel group here in Cincinnati. She sings in the young children's choir at my church and I see me in her all the time. I see what blessings God has given me and I try to pass them on to her, and that makes my heart just glow. I feel as though God is saying to me, "Well done, my faithful servant."

Just the other day a little chubby boy said to me out of the blue, "You know? . . . If I was you, I would just soar to the skies." I was stunned. I *have* been wanting to travel.

One day, out of work and suffering with my backache, I had

had enough. My medicine wasn't working and my pains were so severe, I began to cry. My granddaughter came in the room and began to console me. She said, "Grandma, your back hurt?

"Yes, it does," I said.

"Grandma, remember, you gonna get a new body. You won't have to cry no more. God's gonna give you a new body and we are gonna sit with Him." And then she said, "You are the best grandma I have ever had, and I don't wanna live here without you. When you die, I wanna die too." I thought to myself *Oh, Lawd! This child is something else.* She rubbed my back with her knees, elbows, and feet to make me feel better. God bless that child.

—Lynn Smith

One day, out of the blue, my four-year-old daughter said, "Remember when I was in your belly and I didn't know what you were going to look like?"

A little shocked, I replied, "Yes. And I didn't know what you looked like yet either."

With a wise tone of voice she said, "Well, of course I recognized your voice. I just couldn't see you yet, but I already knew you from before. I chose you, you know."

—Carrie

"**S**weetheart, what are you looking at?" I said.

"I am looking at my message," said Victoria.

"Your message?"

"Yes, my birthday message from God and Jesus."

"Where do you see it?"

"God and Jesus write you a special message each year on the day after your birthday, and it is written in the clouds."

"What does it say?" I asked.

"It is very special and just for me. You will see your message the day after your birthday . . . if you look really hard at the clouds," she answered.

"I always told you that you were a special angel sent to me from God and Jesus."

"Yes . . . I am," said Victoria.

—**Amy Holland**

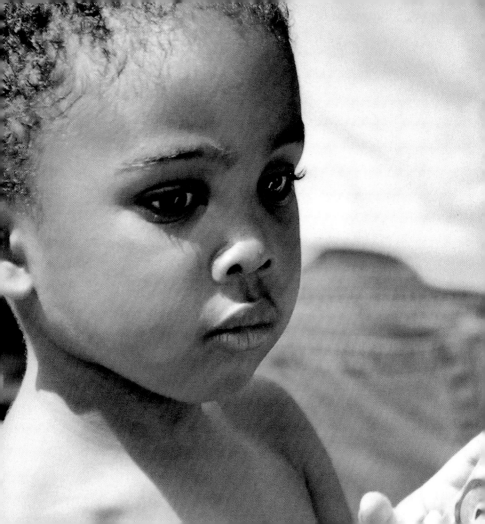

When my boys were young, three years old and eight months old, I heard laughter—the sound of childlike, utter bliss—from their room. I opened the door. **They were both standing facing each other in the center of the room, bare skinned** but for diapers, their eyes and arms reaching upwards. They appeared to be looking and reaching toward a space about two feet below the ceiling. I couldn't see what they were seeing. **When I asked my eldest what he was looking at, he said, "The Man,"** and pointed there at that spot with which they were both so happy (dare I say in ecstasy?). I get chills writing it, but when he said, "The Man," the party was over.

—**Amber Morgan**

My son Jaylan, now eight years old, said "You know, Momma, I always loved you. *I remember when I was with God and told him how much I loved you and wanted to be with you.* So with God, I chose you to be my mother. God said, 'Yes, she will be your mother,' and I came with you." His words brought tears to my eyes and filled my heart with joy; my son understood.

—**Manon Delisle**

My son Justin was born five years after the death of my biological mother Florence. At the time I was still married and my husband's parents were alive and well. By the time he was two, Justin had only known Mi-ma (my husband's mother) by phone and he knew my two godmothers by the names Nana Nikki and Nana C. He had not been taught the word *grandma*; for him it had no reference. **My heart ached that my mother had not lived to see my beautiful son. I shared this feeling with no one! Then one night, as my two-year-**

Blair
Underwood

old was sleeping beside me he became restless. Without breaking his sleep, he said, "Grandma?"

I sat straight up in bed. "Justin, Justin. What did you see?" I asked.

"Grandma," he said as he dropped back off to sleep.

I know that he saw her in his dreams that night. They wanted me to know that they had in fact met and were still in touch. I was the one who wondered.

—LaRita Shelby

My mother passed away a couple of years ago. I have a large family and was assigned the unbearable task of speaking at her funeral. My daughter saw me struggling with what to write for my speech the night before. On the day of the service, before I went before my family, my daughter ran up to me and handed me a letter to read at the funeral. It was entitled "A Letter to Aiya" (*Grandma* in baby talk) This is it:

A Letter to Aiya

She's our Aiya and she'll always be our Aiya. I was so sad when she died, but we shouldn't be sad because we will see her again. I think some people in this room know what this day is, that day is when Jesus comes! Aiya is so unforgettable! We will think of her in our memories, also in our hearts and our minds. If you were at our house last night, I think some of you saw the circle around the moon, that was Aiya! And the stars around her were the angels welcoming her into heaven! After a couple of hours, my cousin and I went to bed and we saw Aiya. We said, "We love you, Aiya" and all the sweetest things we could think of. Thank you!

This letter brought all of my family to tears, even the soldiers and high-ranking officers in the room! It was definitely a gift to listen to my child's soul!

—Milo Levell

One day I took Paris, then seven, and Brielle, then five, to play miniature golf. As we were preparing to leave I made certain that the kids made potty stops before we hit the road for the long ride home. **We had settled in the car and were about to go when I realized that I hadn't made a potty stop for myself.** I explained to them that I needed to do so before we left the golfing grounds. As I prepared to get out of the car, Paris said to me, "Auntie Dottie, you made sure we got our potty break but you didn't remember yours. You must always take care of yourself, Auntie Dottie, 'cause no one else will."

—**Dorothea Barlow**

ne day my four-year-old granddaughter was sitting at the table with her mother, and she asked her mother to buy her a doll. Her mother, who was on public assistance at the time, told her she didn't have any money.

My granddaughter put her hand on the table, turned to her mother, and told her without blinking an eye: "Well, Mother, I think you need to go and get a job so you can get a bank card like Grandma, and go to the bank to take out some money and buy me a doll so Grandma doesn't have to keep doing everything." After that she proceeded to get up from the table and turn to me to say, "Grandma, you don't have to worry, because just like you always tell me I'm going to go to school and college and get a job. Then I will take care of you." Well, my mouth dropped open, and her mother was a little upset to say the least. It amazes me that even today she continues to keep true to her word. At age six she does very well in school.

—**Renee Maceden**

I'm a twenty-five-year-old single parent (the mother of a six-year-old daughter). For as long as I can remember—according to my mom, since I was about four—I repeatedly told her that **"I was an old white woman and I drove my car off a cliff and came back as Rashanda."**

I don't usually share this with anyone other than my family, because I know it sounds crazy. Thank God my mother never took me to a psychiatrist but always listened and supported me. To this day, I can clearly see myself as an old white-haired lady driving a car off of a cliff. And this replays and replays in my mind all the time. I never could see the car actually crash because the vision diminishes in my thoughts. I'm a Southern Baptist and I really do not believe in reincarnation, but there has to be some explanation for my thoughts. I've tried to reason with myself; I've thought that maybe I saw at an early age and had inadvertently incorporated some scene into my memory. **Instead of looking at this terrible event as a movie, I believed it was an incident in my life.** Some of us, as adults, must come to terms with the memories or thoughts that haunt us as children.

I have long been hesitant to tell people for fear that they will think I've flipped my lid. I mostly keep it between my mom and me, but these days we are able to laugh about it. I appreciate the opportunity to write these words and let my soul speak.

—Rashanda Gunter

Two weeks after the birth of my daughter, Ryenne, Elise, one of my friends, had come over to see the new baby. When she picked my baby up, she said, "Oh, my God . . . she has blessings all over her, and **her eyes are so focused and full of love.**" I was a young mom at the time, so my main response was "Thank you." I thought more about what she said after she left, though.

For years after that, every time her picture was taken, she said "I love you" with her eyes. One day she and I were sitting in the living room. I was watching television, and she was building something with her building blocks. Suddenly she stopped building and stared at me. I pretended not to notice her staring because she would say silly things to get my attention. I wanted to hear her say something silly again. But this time she said, "Momma, I'm glad God gave you to me."

I said, "God gave me to you?"

She said, "Yes, ma'am. God said, 'Where do you want to go?' I picked you, and God said, 'Okay.'"

Then she tilted her head to the side, smiled, and nodded at me as if I had just complimented her pretty new dress. Then she resumed building. I wanted to help her build, and I did. My daughter will be thirteen years old this month, and her eyes are still full of love, and she still amazes me. I am still, very much, God's gift to her and she is very much mine.

—Monique Renee Allen

I have four children by my first marriage, ages fifteen, thirteen, ten, and six. More recently, I've found a wonderful husband who has no biological children. We've discussed having a baby several times.

In June 2004, my husband, Jeffery, and my youngest child, Eric, were at the mall shopping. As we passed the infant clothing section, Eric picked up the cutest outfit and asked Jeffrey to buy it, but my husband replied, "We don't have a baby to wear it."

Eric replied instantly, **"If you give Momma more love maybe we can get a baby."** My husband said he was speechless and he laughed out loud as they went on to eat lunch.

—Teresa Easley

was driving in my car a couple of days after my anniversary trip to Miami. **I was depressed about living in the state of Delaware,** and I was talking out loud about how I was going to move to Georgia or Florida. My six-year-old daughter heard me and immediately responded, "Mom, you can't move."

"Why?" I asked.

"Because I love my room and my house. Plus you decorated it so nicely. ***You know God says where he wants you to live and he wants you to live in Delaware, not Georgia nor Florida.***"

I was overwhelmed by her response, and I just paused and smiled to myself. "You're right," I said. "I will live in Delaware until God tells me to live in another state."

—Crystal Robertson

I was putting my five-year-old son, Christiaan, to bed one night after a long day of working in the yard. I had thrown on an old T-shirt to do the yardwork, and hadn't paid any attention to the writing on it.

I was rushing him to bed because it was already past his bedtime and time had gotten away from me. Then, out of nowhere, he looked at me with awe and said, **"Mommy, where did you get that shirt?"**

"I don't know. I found it in the drawer—maybe Grandma gave it to me," I replied.

"Oh, Mommy, that is so true, God has been sooo good to me. He is totally awesome. He loves me and

Blair **Underwood**

he whispers for me to wake up on mornings."

My shirt had an iron-on that read GOD HAS BEEN SO GOOD TO ME. We aren't regular churchgoers, and I truly don't know where it came from. The whole chain of events had an eerily spiritual side to it, and Christiaan took on a different look and a very serious voice that night, as if **God truly was speaking through him.** I kissed my son and I took the time to lie down with him in my arms until he fell asleep. It was as if God was saying, "Stop a moment and enjoy and appreciate the gifts I have given you."

—Donovan Branche

My six-year-old daughter Alyssa loves to draw pictures for me. One Sunday morning Alyssa walked up to me, showed me a picture, and said, **"Look, Mommy, I made you a picture of Jesus and his angels. God gave the three angels a crown and Jesus is on the cross and the fire is under the angels, but there is light over Jesus."**

I was in awe. And I said, "How did you know to draw this?"

"I just know," she replied.

Later when Alyssa was asleep she woke up in the middle of the night and asked me why the angels and everybody called her Tabatha. After that she lay back down in the bed and went to sleep. **I asked Alyssa the next day if she remembered saying this to me,** and she did not. I believe her to be spiritually gifted because she speaks a lot about angels, life, what happens after death, and what will happen when Jesus comes back.

—Anisha Moorer

My daughter Lauren has been and is always fascinated by people with moles. One day Lauren told me that she liked moles because that is where God has kissed someone. I asked her how she knew, and she said God had told her. I asked her to tell me some of the things God had told her. *She said that God had told her all about me and what I would look like, and even about her brother and sister.* I asked her what God looked like, and she said she can remember but she can't find the words to tell me. I gave her crayons and paper and asked her to draw a picture, and she drew a large heart on the paper.

—Michele Scott Flores

My six-year-old nephew Jordeyn Lewis has a glow about him that is indescribable. **He often says things that amaze me,** and I could probably write a book about the various comments he makes. I have often found myself gazing at him in amazement for quite some time not only at what he says but the look in his eyes. **Nothing can describe the look in a child's eyes,** for it conveys so many things beyond what children can explain to us. Their eyes have the power to make us laugh, cry, or smile for days.

"If God wants us to be good then why do we do bad things?" "Is Jesus still on the cross?" "Want to be a teacher when I grow up so people will listen." "Why doesn't everyone have a mommy?"—Jordeyn

—Audrey De Shong

My three-year-old nephew, Justin, had a very close relationship with my father. Whenever Justin came to visit, if he didn't see my father when he walked in the door, he'd make a beeline to his grandfather's bedroom. My father passed away in November. **For weeks afterward when Justin came to visit, he'd still race through my house looking for "Granddad."** Finally, Justin's parents explained to him that Granddad wouldn't be coming back.

Recently on a beautiful spring evening Justin and I were sitting on our front porch. Out of the blue, Justin tapped me on my leg and said, "Auntie, I know where Granddad is."

"Oh? Where is he?" I asked.

"He's in the moon and the stars,"

Justin replied. He then pointed to the bright moon and said, "Look, there he is. Granddad is inside that shiny one up there!"

"Who told you that?" I asked.

"Nobody, I told my own self," he said.

"How do you know Granddad is in the shiny one?" I asked.

He smiled really wide and said, *"Because God is in there with Granddad,* and that's how Granddad got shiny." I took Justin in my arms and cried. I was so grateful because this little boy's perspective on my dad's passing was the catalyst that helped me to heal from the grief.

—**Audrey Forman**

My daughter Laura was about three or four years old when she told me about "her husband" who died in the water. I asked her what happened to him and whether he was swimming.

She said they were on a boat with a lot of people real close together and they (she didn't say who "they" were) threw him off the boat. I asked her if she dreamed that and she said, "No. My husband died, but I didn't."

—Janice Shannon

Blair Underwood

When my son (and only child) was three years old, he began to speak of a sister named Sarah. He would not eat a meal without placing food out for Sarah, and each evening he would prepare a place for her to sleep in his bed. **He included her in every aspect of our lives.** I would inquire about who she was and where she lived. He insisted that she was his sister and that she resided with us. He would stop in midsentence to ask her opinion. He insisted that she was present until he was in the early months of his sixth year. *He will turn eight years old on New Year's Eve, and he still occasionally speaks of her.*

He also speaks extremely fondly of my husband's deceased father. My husband's father made the transition roughly fourteen years before my son's birth. During the same period that he communicated with Sarah, he also communicated with my husband's father (of whom my husband never speaks). **He is an extremely mystical child**. I have referred to him as my little spirit since his conception. He confirms my belief that energy cannot be destroyed; it can only change form.

—Edith Richardson

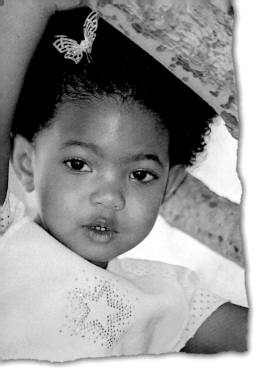

was twenty-two years old when I became pregnant with my daughter, Latoya, and as an unwed mother-to-be, I **was reluctant to tell my mother I had messed up.** The man by whom I was pregnant was a professional boxer and had many problems with telling the truth, so I knew marriage was not going to be an option for me. I had been raised in a Christian home and I am the granddaughter of a bishop in the African Methodist Episcopal Church, so **I knew I would instantly become the "black sheep" of the family. I can remember lying in the bathtub weeping as I confessed to my mother that I was pregnant.**

When my daughter was four or five years old, she said that she saw me the day I was in the bathtub talking to my mother. I was flabbergasted to hear this. No one but my mother could have told her about that day, and my daughter recalled it with such conviction and clarity you would think she had literally been in the bathroom with us.

—Beatrice Johnson

Arthur, my beloved Brittany spaniel, had to be sent away immediately. I had nurtured and loved him since he was a mere pup, and **with one terrible act I was forced to choose my child over him.** Having struck my son's face with his canine teeth so deep that the plastic surgeon later told me that the dog hit the tender bone just centimeters from my little boy's eye, I was left with no choice.

In the emergency room on his thirteen-month birthday, I held my son in my arms as his face wept drops of blood. Rocking his gentle body, we waited as one for the pediatric plastic surgeon to arrive. His little arm pricked and readied for the anesthesiologist, I was sent away. **A part of me couldn't stop crying over losing my dog.** There I sat nervously suspended until the anesthesia wore off and Philip's blue eyes regained their brilliance.

Hours turned into days as **Philip's face started the slow healing process that would leave a telltale scar that I was assured would fade along with his childhood.** The physical wound on his face worried me less than the possible psychological impact the trauma might have caused.

In my dog-loving neighborhood people and pooches share the sidewalks, so a doggie encounter is a daily occurrence. With the bandage only removed from his swollen face, it was time for a walk in the buggy. We weren't but six feet from the house when I eyed a man and his Labrador retriever pup approaching. **Before I could tell him the story and why I wanted him to stay away, the puppy had jumped up on Philip and quickly licked his face several times.** Philip giggled like it tickled. There was no holding back little Philip's excitement. Struggling to break free from his safety harness, he suddenly vocalized, "Oggie. Oggie. Wow!" His hands pointed as his mouth clacked with happiness. I dared to free him from the stroller knowing how much he would scream once I tried to get him back into it. Nevertheless, on wobbly legs Philip embraced the pup's enthusiasm. **That was the first time I understood what my mother had meant when she talked about the beauty of children's innocence and the unconditional love that they feel.** Philip wasn't holding any grudges against dogs or calculating another route through life hoping to avoid any canine meetings. He had already forgotten about what had happened and moved on with enjoying life.

—Diane de Castro

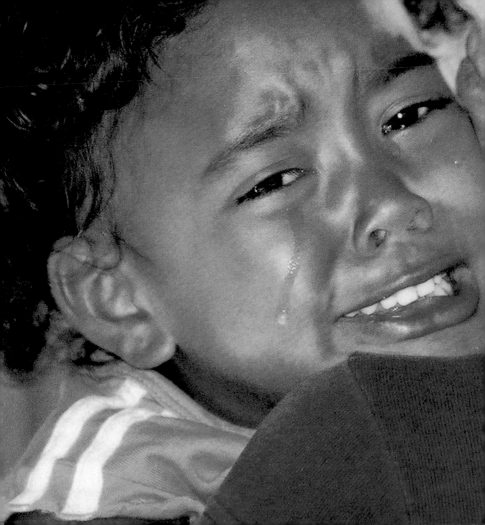

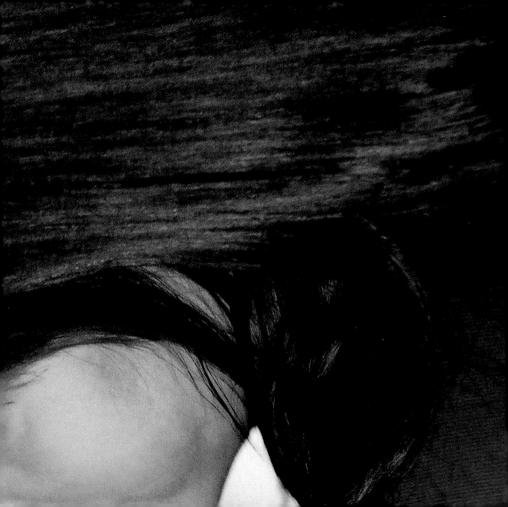

One day, as I drove my daughter Cherish home from day care, she spoke about the clouds and how beautiful Heaven was. **I asked her how she knew Heaven was so beautiful.**

Cherish told me she knew because she lived there before she was born. She then told me that God loved her and knew how much I had wanted a daughter, so He sent her here for me.

—**Daphne Mcdonald**

When my daughter was about four or five years old she told me that she was the reason my husband and I were married. I asked her what she meant and she said, "Mommy, when I was in Heaven before I was born, I saw you and told God I wanted you for my mommy. Then I saw Daddy and said that's who I wanted for my father. *So God let you two meet and love each other and get married so you could both be my parents."* She will be sixteen years old this summer and still reminds us of this from time to time.

—Nancy Williams

have two daughters: Julliette, who will soon turn six, and Paloma, who will turn three. I call them my sun and moon children, respectively. Their personalities are as different from one another as their names.

Julliette has always had an innate connection to God, the spirit world, and in particular, my late father and my husband's late mother. They both died before our children were born. *Julliette, however, "speaks" to them frequently and often cries about missing them.* My husband and I are both spiritual; he firmly believes in God, but I have struggled with that concept since events in my life made me feel somewhat betrayed by Him. This fact is of particular relevance because Julliette, it seems, often speaks to me about God as if helping to guide me back to trust that name again.

One day when my husband was out of town I had a very tense and stress-filled afternoon, which culminated with my raising my voice and feeling not so good about it afterward. I put Paloma to bed and read a book to Julliette. I then took a few moments, held her little hand, and said, "I'm sorry that I was upset tonight, Julliette. I don't like yelling at you guys. Mommy's just tired."

"It's okay," she said. Her "okays" always take my breath away.

Then, as if to change the subject for me, she said, "You know who the superhero is?"

"The superhero?" I asked

"It starts with a G."

Trying to imagine things from Julliette's perspective, I asked "God?"

"Yup," she replied. *"You know, He takes care of everybody and makes everything all right."*

"You're right, sweetheart. You're right." I tucked her in, told her I loved her, and then she went to sleep. That night I was quite moved by what she'd said and of course the profundity of her timely wisdom. The next morning, I told her that what she had said had really made me feel better. I told her it helped me get a good night's sleep.

"Mommy, I can tell you that and you'll always have a good sleep," she responded. I cried and smiled and hugged her like I never wanted to let her go.

—Alexis Stripling

My daughter, Kianna, has always been a creative, intellectual, logical child. **There have been many conversations between us in the thirteen years I have been blessed to have her in my life.** One such conversation occurred after the death of her grandfather.

We lived across the street from my mother and stepfather at the time of his death from prostate cancer. Kianna was only four years old at the time. She was very attached to him and everyone was concerned about how his passing would affect her. I decided to take Kianna to the funeral home to view the body, much to many of my relatives' chagrin. She walked right up to her beloved granddaddy, leaned very, very close to his face and studied it carefully. She asked me,

"Mommy, is he asleep?"

I responded, "No, honey, he is not alive anymore."

"Does it hurt?" she asked.

"No, honey," I said.

"Is he with Jesus?"

"Yes, Jesus will take care of him now," I told her.

After much thought, Kianna took my hand, ready to leave.

Later that day, I saw her looking out our front window up at the sky. I asked her what she was looking at, and she said, ***"I'm looking for Granddaddy because he is a blessing in 'the skies' now."*** She had overheard people saying that her grandfather's death was a blessing "in disguise" because he wasn't suffering anymore. I thought that was a wonderful way for her to think of her grandfather.

—Donna Davis

Before I Got Here

One morning while sitting at the breakfast table, I was having a quick breakfast with Xia, my one-year-old daughter, and Koi, my two-year-old daughter. Exhausted by lack of sleep and early morning duties, I gazed into my bowl of fruit, wondering how I could keep up without getting burned out. The girls were humming (their daily eating hum) while eating cereal and fruit. Suddenly, to my amazement, the room got quiet and Koi said in a sweet and clear voice, **"Mommy, I love you."** At that moment, I realized the power of thought and how my children appreciate and understand my love. Moments like that give me strength to jump any hurdle.

—**Elva Anderson**

W hen she was three years old, on one morning as I drove her to school, my oldest daughter Fallon asked me a question: "Mommy, when I was in your stomach as a baby, could I see through your eyes?"

I asked her from where her question came. She told me that she remembered looking through my eyes at my reflection in a mirror while she was still inside me. **She said that she remembered that I was rubbing my stomach and singing her a song** and that it sounded so pretty that she decided to stay there until she could come see me. I was absolutely amazed, because one of my favorite things to do while I was pregnant was to stand in front of a mirror and admire the changes in myself while rubbing my stomach and humming songs to my baby. Fallon also told me that she picked me to be her mommy. This conversation has never left my thoughts and I have often wondered *Did she choose me? Is it possible?*

At the time, I couldn't imagine that a child of three could have created such a story, but ***she has proven to be an amazingly soulful child.*** She reaches out to everyone with laughter, joy, kindness, and often very insightful thoughts and messages that are much older than she.

—**Tammy Barros**

"Il never forget an experience I had with my son when he was eight years old. We were driving in a storm, when suddenly the rain stopped but the sky remained very dark and cloudy. Then, out of the blue, my eight-year-old said, "Look, Mom, the pretty lady. Look at all the colors around her."

I looked and saw nothing, but the expression on his face was so peaceful and sincere. I questioned him and he continued to say, "Just look at her,

Mom, and stop talking." I kept questioning him, and he responded by telling me more about what she looked like, the colors around her, and the pretty smile on her face. When I got home I asked him to draw for me what he saw. To this day I still have his picture of what looks like the Virgin Mary. I still ask him from time to time about that evening, and he still insists on what he saw. I only wish I could have seen it, too.

—Patricia

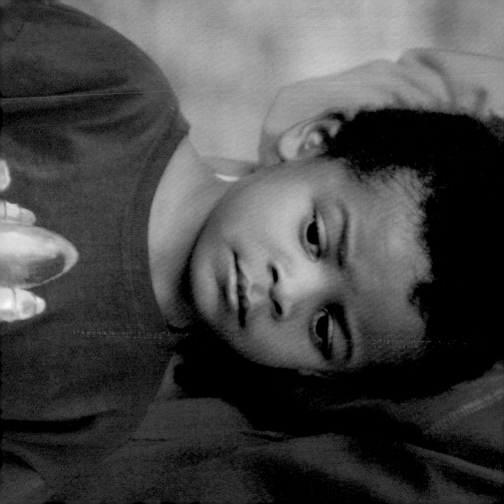

I t was one month after Paul, my dear firstborn, died (he passed away just thirty-eight days prior to his fifteenth birthday). Matthew, my second child, was only five at the time and trying to cope by God's grace. Matthew came to me and said, **"Mommy, I dreamed that Paul came to take me to Heaven and he was stretching his hand out to take me up,** and I was stretching to go up to him. We were so happy, and a voice said out of Heaven gently, 'No, let him stay with your mom,' and then I woke up." Matthew was happy to see Paul happy, and I was happy to have Matt with me. He's now sixteen with many more years to come. I can never forget this soul sharing with my son.

—Patricia R. Blackwood

My niece passed away on August 8, 2004, at the age of twenty-nine. Her four-year-old son told her a month prior to her death that "my momma is going to die." Of course, my niece was scared and shaken by his remarks, but I believe it was a sign from God through her son to let her know that her time was near.

—Christine Freeland

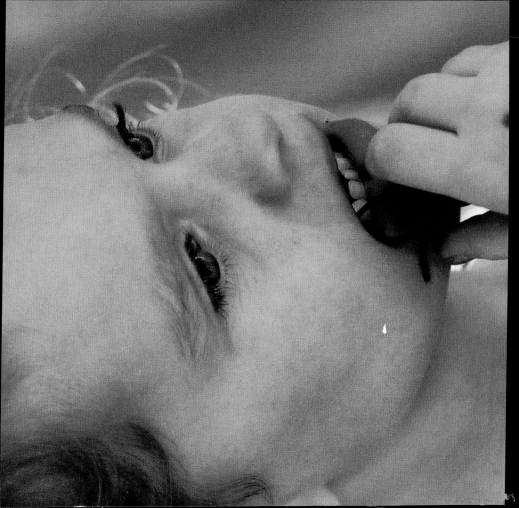

Every morning my son Hunter has his usual bowl of cereal at his table before he gets ready for school. One particular morning while eating he looked up from his bowl and said to me, **"Mommy, what is it like to be my mother?"** Needless to say, I was quite taken aback by such a profound statement and thought, *Wow! Where did that come from?* I will never forget the expression on his face when he asked me this. This was definitely from my son's soul!

—Leigh Brown

had really bad luck last year trying to conceive another child. I was just about to lose my fourth when I had an amazing conversation with my daughter McKenna.

"Honey, Mommy needs to have a serious conversation with you. It concerns the new baby on the way. After tomorrow I won't be pregnant anymore."

Without missing a beat she said to me, **"Ah, no fair for you, Mommy. Hey, tell you what, the next baby you and I will make together. And we'll put tape all over it."**

I was baffled by that comment and said, "What for, honey?" At three years old, her answer was, "That way this one will stick." At three years old she knew these babies weren't "sticking" somehow.

When McKenna was two years old a psychic had told me how "special" she was. *She told me she would be asking for a baby brother,* and that evening she did. That is probably why I tried so hard to get pregnant . . . for her. You see, my sister Karla died when I was nine and she was thirteen. She was my best friend in the universe. After watching my parents suffer as a result of her death, I felt that I'd never want any kids. Ultimately I realized that my sister, like an angel, had everything in the world to do with having this child. I realized that life is destiny and **one has to go through everything and experience whatever is intended.** I also realized that the spirit is made up of energy; you can't kill energy, it just changes form, thereby becoming the soul. I have such a special gift in my daughter. We teach each other so much every day. Some days she is so much wiser than I am. McKenna Karly Thurber is truly my little soulmate. It's so wonderful to have made your best friend.

—Paula Trickey

It was a morning just like any other. My four-year-old son Brandon was talking and asking questions while I finished dressing his two-year-old brother Cameron. As Brandon played his usual game of fifty questions, he reminded me, as gently as a four-year-old can, **"I am talking to you Mom, you need to listen . . . HELLO!"**

Cameron and I shared a laugh and then we turned our full attention to Brandon. "Mom, Opa is in Heaven?" This must have been the umpteenth time he asked that question, staring at the photo collage of Opa (Dutch for Grandpa) that we made for him.

"Yes, Brandon." I answered. "Opa was very old and sick. When he died he went to Heaven."

Cameron chimed in, "Opa's in Heaven, Bran."

And then Brandon put his little hand on his baby brother's shoulder and said, "Yes, Cam, Opa's in Heaven. *He loved you very much, then he was dead 'cause he was sick.* He went to Heaven, okay? His body stayed here and got burned up to dust, but his soul went to Heaven. And they put the dust in a pretty bottle. I don't want to go to Heaven, Cam, because I don't want to die, okay?"

"Okay," answered Cameron.

"And my soul is going to stay in my body so I won't get burnt up, okay, Cam? You don't want to get burnt up, do you, Cam?" said Brandon.

"No, it's too hot, don't touch, owie!" answered Cameron.

Oh, my heart! I didn't know what to say. Brandon was speaking so gently to his little brother and so profound was his reasoning, I couldn't bring myself to correct him. Yes, we still talk about life, death, and Heaven, and I know one day the two of them will understand it the way grown folks do. But for now, I curb my instinct to guide through correction and I listen and watch in amazement.

—E. Monique Floyd Sapp

My son was eleven as we were driving on Route 95 from Baltimore to New York City. We had a close call with a truck, and I commented that *"We were almost history."* He was in the backseat and I sensed he was upset.

Teary-eyed, he said, "Science is great, but if you just believe in science, then when you die you die. If you believe in God, there's something more than this life."

—Helen Dunne

I lost my firstborn son, Patrick, in a car accident in 1982. My baby boy, Kevin, was four years old at the time. Each time Kevin asked about his brother, I would tell him that Patrick was in Heaven with God. **One day we were raking leaves in the yard and he kept looking up at the clouds.** I asked him what he was thinking about. He said "Patrick." Tears welled up in my eyes as he continued, "I hope Pat's doing good in Heaven, 'cause if God has to kick him out, he'll break his neck when he hits the ground." Needless to say my tears turned into laughter.

—Janet Day

When my son Miles was about three years old, we were living in East Harlem, New York. One day while I was washing the dishes, Miles sat on the counter next to me. Out of the blue, he started to tell me about his old life. As he watched me wash dishes, he told me that I reminded him of his "other mother" who used to do so. I was slightly taken aback, but I wasn't startled, nor did I want to startle him. Our conversation proceeded.

"My other mother used to do that," Miles said.

"Oh, really? Who is your other mother?" I said.

"She's not here now. She's dead. She died a long time ago," he replied in a nonchalant tone.

"Oh, okay, I'm sorry, baby," I said.

"She was really nice. She used to read to me and she would sit with me, too, just like this."

"Oh, that's so nice," I replied.

"But she's gone now, you're my new mommy now. You're nice, too," he said.

"Well, I'm glad to be your new mommy, but tell me more about your old mommy."

"I don't remember her that good anymore. I could remember a lot before, but now I don't. I can't see her good anymore in here [he pointed to his head]. You're the new mommy now."

"Okay, well that's fine by me."

"It's fine by me, too, Mommy."

Miles is seventeen years old now, and my conversations with him have always been amazing.

—**Sonya Perkins**

Before I
Got Here   161

When my niece was three years old, she came to visit me at work. She asked me to take her to the restroom, so I grabbed hold of her hand and led her down the hallway. As we were walking she looked up to me and said, **"One day you are going to cry over all your sins."**

Shocked by what she said and not believing what I heard, I asked her to repeat what she said. She repeated, "One day you are going to cry over all your sins." My niece is now thirteen years old.

—Charlene Denton

After losing my oldest son in a drowning accident, my two other sons and I moved into another apartment in a new neighborhood. Upon moving in I felt all alone, especially with the absence of my oldest son. One evening as I looked out the window I **noticed a distinctive star shining directly into my bedroom.** Almost immediately something inside of me told me that that star was for me. That star was my oldest son's sign, showing me that he was watching over me, and immediately I felt overwhelmingly safe and secure.

I never mentioned this to my youngest son Paul. One evening, much later, Paul came into my room and asked me how I felt. Before I could reply, he said to me, "You'll be all right."

I said, "How do you know?"

He looked up to the window and turned to me and replied, "See that star?" while pointing to my secret star.

"Yes, I see it, Paul," I said.

"Well, that's Cedric," he said. Cedric is the name of my deceased son. "He's looking at you to make sure you're okay."

Since age three, Paul has said extraordinary things. Once, I told him to put on his slippers and he turned to me and replied, "I'm tired of wearing slippers." I asked him why he was tired of wearing slippers, and he replied **"I wore slippers for sixty-five years when I was here before."**

I also remember the time he told me that when he was in the sky with God he saw me looking sad. He asked God if I could be his mother so I'd no longer have to be sad, and God said yes. It is a pleasure to be Paul's mother, and he never ceases to amaze me with the things that he says.

—Carlise Florence

used to live on the sixth floor of a housing project in Queens, New York, overlooking the Manhattan skyline. It was difficult to see very much because of the safety guards on the windows, but it was a pretty nice view. **Every now and then police helicopters would fly over and the buzz would create a lot of noise because we were on the top floor.** My son Justin, who was maybe four or five at the time, heard a helicopter flying over our building one night, and he climbed up to the window to see it. But for some reason, this copter wasn't moving. It was just hovering overhead for a very long time. **The noise drew me to the window, and my son and I sat there looking at it in silence for a long time.** Frustrated, I asked aloud, "I wonder why he's just sitting there, not going anywhere."

That's when my baby said to me, with the patience of an old soul, "Mommy, maybe he just stopped to ask God for directions."

—Audrey M. Gabourel

O
ne evening when my daughter was four years old we were walking home from day care. I looked up and discovered that the moon was out and completely round. I exclaimed, "Wow! There's a full moon out tonight!" **My daughter looked up and I could see that she was deep in thought.**

Suddenly, she stopped, pulled my hand, and asked, "How come the moon is full? Did it eat a sandwich?" I hugged her and explained to her what I meant when I said that the moon was full. She did not get the meaning, but I had a better understanding of her views and understanding about her world of words.

—**Michelle Borden**

When my daughter Shameka was about four, we sat at home one day, when out of nowhere she said, **"I'm not like everyone else. I'm different."** I asked her what she meant. She said, "I've been here before." She then asked me whether I have noticed it, and so I began to wonder, Is it possible?

—Essie Graham

When my youngest daughter was about two years old, she would **point to the living room window, waving and talking to someone she would call La La.** She did this constantly. When I would ask her where La La was, she would say "right there," but of course, I saw nothing. I would call my husband and he couldn't see her either. I still wonder who La La is. *To this very day my daughter, who is now eleven years old, still tells me she sees things*, like my mother who passed away.

—Essie Graham

Dana, five years old, was a petite but feisty young girl with glittering gray eyes and **an unquenchable zest for life.**

One blistering afternoon in the summer of 1996 near her home in Irving, Texas, Dana sat in her mother's lap in the bleachers of a local ballpark where her brother Dustin's baseball team was practicing. As always, Dana was chattering nonstop with her mother and several other adults sitting nearby when she suddenly fell silent.

Hugging her arms across her chest, little Dana asked, "Do you smell that?"

Smelling the air and detecting the approach of a thunderstorm, her mother Diana replied, "Yes, it smells like rain."

Dana closed her eyes and again asked, "Do you smell that?"

Once again, her mother replied, "Yes, I think we're about to get wet. It smells like rain."

Still caught in the moment, Dana shook her head, patted her thin shoulders with her small hands, and loudly announced, **"No, it smells like Him. It smells like God when you lay your head on His chest."**

—Nancy Parente

editor's note

Feel free to log onto www.BeforeIGotHere.com, and submit the amazing and spiritual things your children say.

your children's sayings